I AM...
WHO GOD SAYS I AM

BY: Jerry & Laetitia BONSU

ILLUSTRATED BY: Alvin V.Cadiz
Copyright 2014 Jerry Bonsu and Laetitia Bonsu

Published by Victory Life Media an imprint of JBM
JERRY BONSU MINISTRIES
Visit our websit: www.jerrybonsu.org

Printed in the U.S.A
French National Library-in- Publication Data
Dépôt légal: 12/2014

ISBN : 978-2-9541960-5-3

For further information or permission, contact us on the internet:
Victory Life Media "Empowering our Generation for the next
Generation" www.victorylifemedia.com

VICTORY LIFE
MEDIA

DEDICATION

To Janelle and Janessa... Each of you are so fearfully and wonderfully made. We look forward to the wonderful works that our Heavenly Father will work through you.

To Aunt Stephanie! Because of God's love there is no one more than you. You are SPECIAL!

INTRODUCTION

Hello! My name is Janelle Kierra Bonsu and this is my little sister Janessa Kimani Bonsu, Our friends call us "Kiki & Kemi". We are very happy that you are going to read this book: I AM WHO GOD SAY I AM, Biblical Affirmations, written by our parents!!!

An affirmation is a compliment that you give to yourself. ....Do you know that the God of the entire universe, the GREAT I AM knows your name? And He calls you friend?!

God said in His Book (The Bible) that He has a great plan for your life. A very BIG plan! with joy, peace, and love.

Read the wonderful words He says about you. Repeat them, and get ready to feel good, better, special, and UNIQUE!

Aa is for Amazing

I am amazing. I am what God says I am.
Chosen by Jesus, named by Jesus
Saved in Jesus, always with Jesus.
I am blessed, you see
I am, amazing me.

Bb is for Beautiful

I am beautiful.
I am beautiful, inside and outside.
I am fearfully and wonderfully made.
I am blessed, you see
I am, beautiful me.

Cc is for **Courageous**

I am courageous. I am Bold.
With God I am fearless.
I can do all things through Christ who strengthens me.
I am blessed, you see
I am, courageous me.

Dd is for Destined

I am destined.
Destined for greatness, destined for success.
God has a perfect plans for my life,
plans to give me hope and a future.
I am blessed, you see
I am, destined me.

Ee is for Enough

I am enough. I am whole and complete.
I am who God says I am, I have what God says I have
And I can do what God says I can.
I am blessed, you see
I am, enough me

Ff is for **Free**

I am free. Free to be me.
I am free from fear, I am free from doubt.
Where the Spirit of the Lord is, there is freedom.
I am blessed, you see
I am, free me

Gg is for Generous

I am generous. I am cheerful giver.
I believe it is better to give than to receive.
I love seeing people happy.
I am blessed, you see
I am, generous me

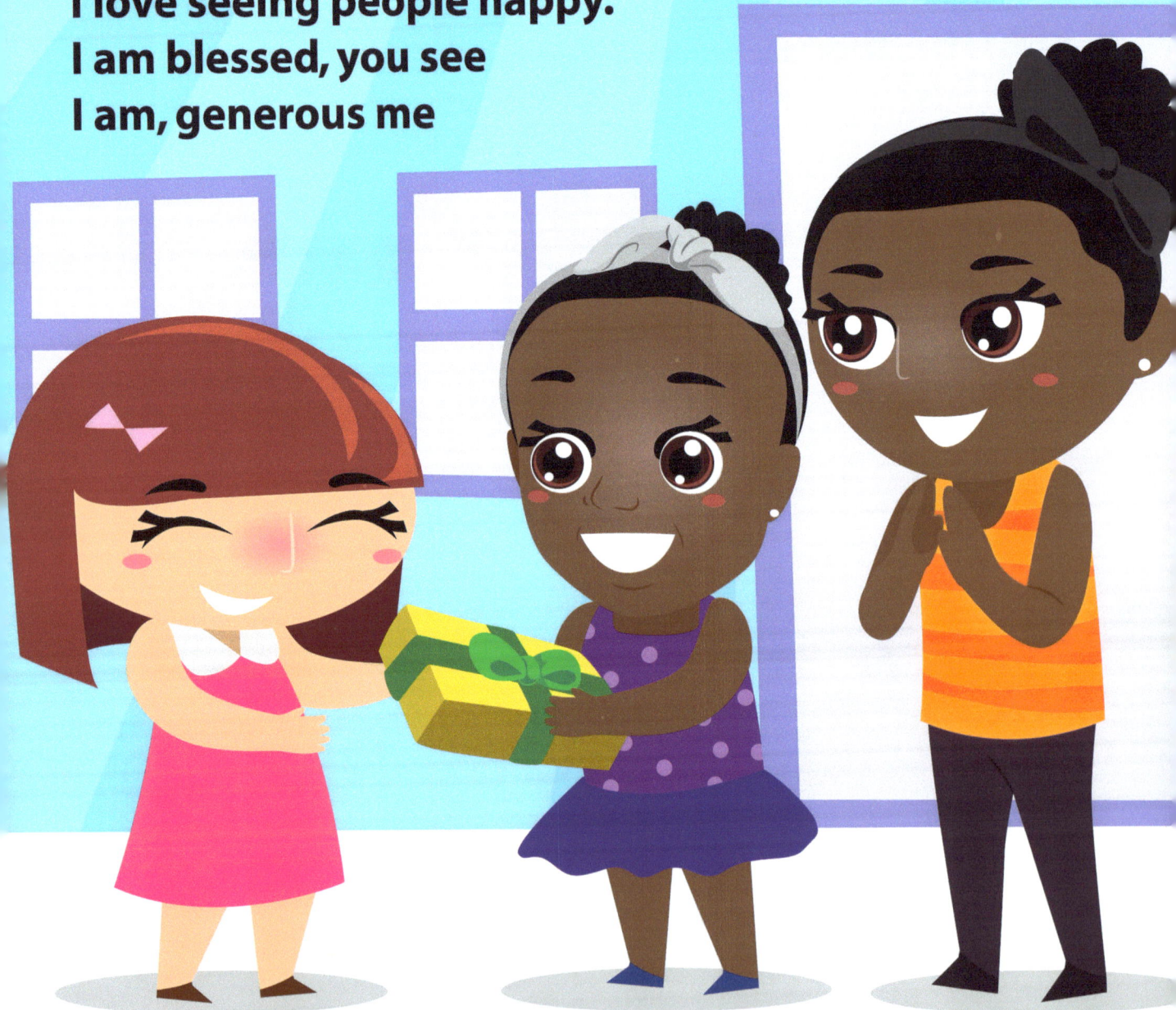

Hh is for Happy

I am happy. Happy to be me.
I am in charge of how I feel and today
I am choosing happiness.
The joy of the Lord is my strength.
I am blessed, you see
I am, happy me.

Ii is for Intelligent

I am intelligent.
God is my source of understanding,
knowledge and wisdom.
I work with excellence. I give 100%, and nothing less.
I am blessed, you see
I am, intelligent me.

Jj is for Joyful

I am joyful. God is my joy, my comfort, and my all.
In His presence, there is fullness of joy.
He puts gladness in my heart everyday.
I am blessed, you see
I am, joyful me.

Kk is for Kind

I am kind. I am friendly to all.
I radiate love and compassion.
I love God and I love people.
I am blessed, you see
I am, kind me

Ll is for **Love**

I am love. I am loved.
Honoured, and treasured by Jesus.
My family, friends and teachers love me for who I am.
I am blessed, you see
I am, love me.

Mm is for Miracle

I am miracle.
I thank God for blessing me with life every day.
I am a blessing to my generation.
I am blessed, you see
I am, miracle me.

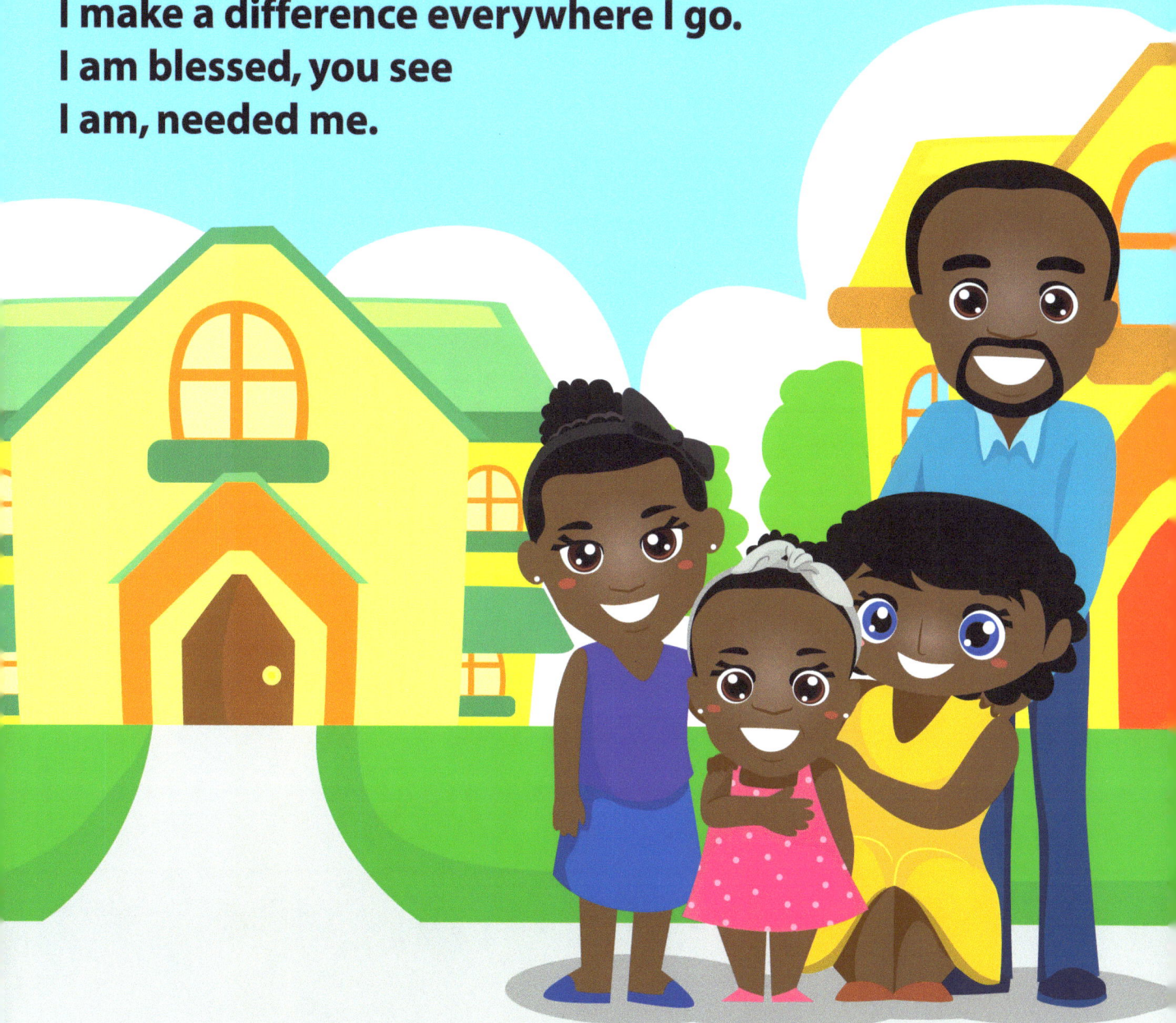

Nn is for Needed

I am needed.
Needed by my family, my friends, my school,
and my community.
I make a difference everywhere I go.
I am blessed, you see
I am, needed me.

Oo is for **Obedient**

I am obedient.
I obey God. I obey my parents in all things.
God says: "Children, obey your parents in the Lord:
for this is right."
I am blessed, you see
I am, obedient me.

Pp is for Precious

I am precious.
Though others may reject me, God sees me as precious.
Yes! I am precious in His sight.
I am blessed, you see
I am, precious me.

Qq is for Queen

I am queen. I am also a princess.
My Father is the King of kings and Lord of lords.
Yes! I am a part of the royal family of God.
I am blessed, you see
I am, queen me.

Rr is for Respectful

I am respectful.
I treat other people the way I want to be treated.
I show caring and respect for others through good manners.
I am blessed, you see
I am, respectful me.

Ss is for Strong

I am strong.
In Christ I am more than a conqueror.
He has changed me into a champion, enabling me to do exploits in His Name.
I am blessed, you see
I am, strong me.

Tt is for Thankful

I am thankful. I am also grateful.
I am grateful that God's plan for my life has never changed.
I am grateful for the favor of God that is on my life.
I am blessed, you see
I am, thankful me.

Uu is for Unique

I am unique. I am also special and valuable.
God designed me the way I am for a purpose.
Everything about me is unique and everything about me matters.
I am blessed, you see
I am, unique me.

Vv

is for **Victorious**

I am victorious.
I am an overcomer in Jesus.
I have the mind of a winner, the heart of a champion, the spirit of a conqueror.
I am blessed, you see
I am, victorious me.

Ww is for Wise

I am wise. I am wise in Christ Jesus.
I am full of the wisdom of God.
And that wisdom is in my heart and in my mouth.
I am blessed, you see
I am, wise me.

Xx is for Xtraordinary

I am eXtraordinary.
God made me perfect in every way.
I am eXceptional.
I am blessed, you see
I am, extraordinary me.

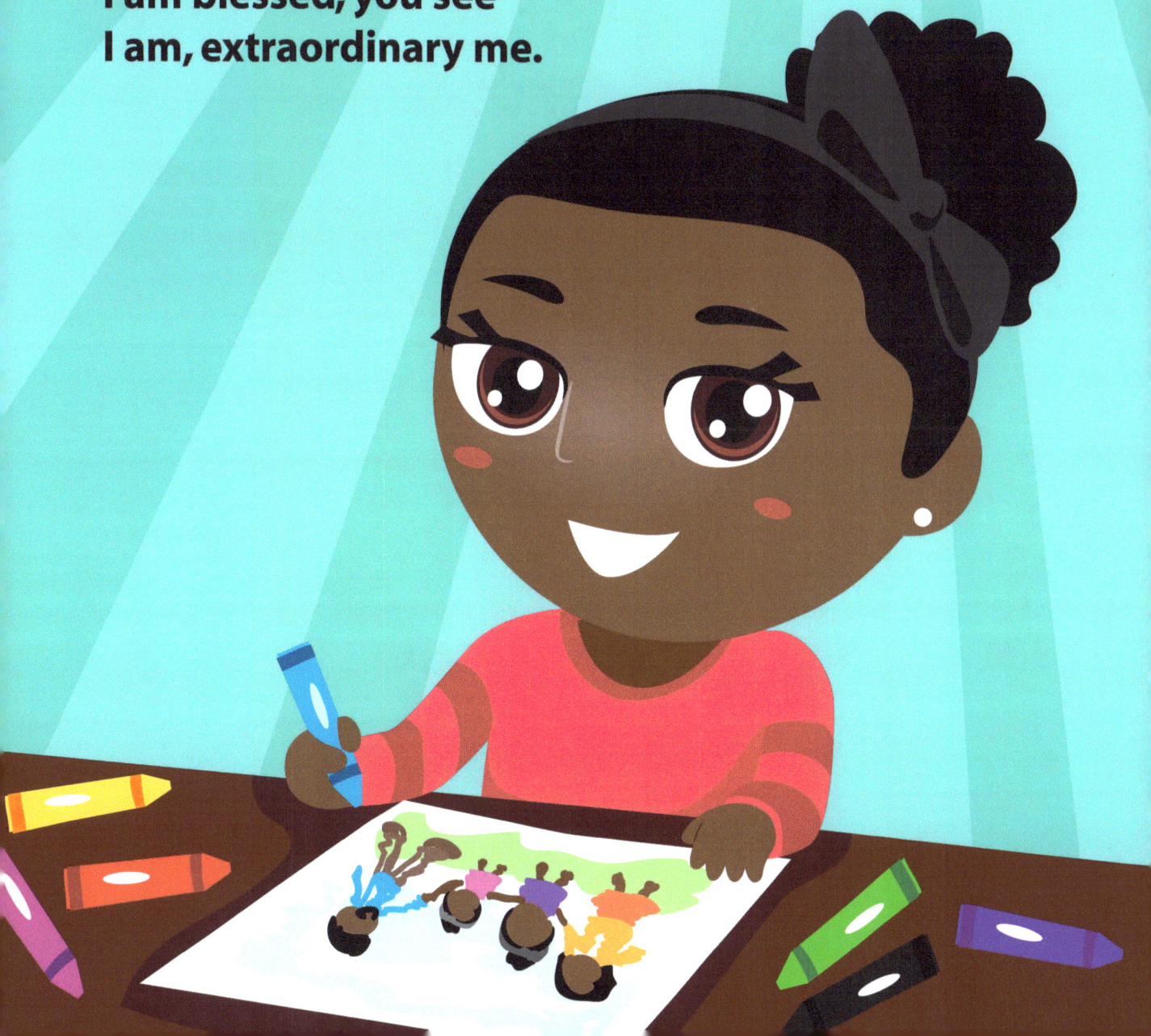

Yy is for Yearning

I am Yearning
Yearning for God, yearning for Jesus, yearning for Holy Spirit
That is why I read my Bible and pray everyday
I am blessed, you see
I am, yearning me

HOLY BIBLE

Zz is for Zealous

I am zealous, zealous for God and His kingdom
I love God with all my heart, with all my soul and with all my mind
I thank God for loving me first
I am blessed, you see
I am, zealous me

www.ingramcontent.com/pod-product-compliance
Lightning Source LLC
Chambersburg PA
CBHW042107040426
42448CB00002B/177